MY DOG

Me and My PET

By William Anthony

KidHaven PUBLISHING

Published in 2020 by KidHaven Publishing, an Imprint of Greenhaven Publishing, LLC
353 3rd Avenue, Suite 255, New York, NY 10010

© 2020 Booklife Publishing

This edition is published by arrangement with Booklife Publishing.

Written by: William Anthony
Edited by: Robin Twiddy
Designed by: Jasmine Pointer

Cataloging-in-Publication Data

Names: Anthony, William.
Title: My dog / William Anthony.
Description: New York : KidHaven Publishing, 2020. | Series: Me and my pet | Includes glossary and index.
Identifiers: ISBN 9781534533370 (pbk.) | ISBN 9781534533394 (library bound) | ISBN 9781534533387 (6 pack) | ISBN 9781534533400 (ebook)
Subjects: LCSH: Dogs--Juvenile literature.
Classification: LCC SF426.5 A58 2020 | DDC 636.7--dc23

Photo credits: Images are courtesy of Shutterstock.com. With thanks to Getty Images, Thinkstock Photo and iStockphoto.
Front cover - African Studio, Amared Metawisai. 2 - Africa Studio. 3 - Fabian Faber, Andrew Burgess. 4 - Africa Studio. 5 - Africa Studio.
6 - BIGANDT.COM. 7 - Monika Chodak. 8 - Pressmaster. 9 - Happy monkey, Nikolai Tsvetkov, Erik Lam. 10 - vvvita. 11 - Hollysdogs.
12 - Africa Studio, 9dream studio. 13 - Nicole Lienemann. 14 - Oleksandr Lysenko. 15 - Yobab. 16 - Pressmaster. 17 - Syda Productions.
18 - Anna Hoychuk. 19 - Nestor Rizhniak. 20 - Wasitt Hemwaraporchai. 21 - Algirdas Mazeika. 22 - Africa Studio. 23 - ESB Professional.

Printed in the United States of America

CPSIA compliance information: Batch #BW20KL: For further information contact Greenhaven Publishing LLC, New York, New York at 1-844-317-7404.

CONTENTS

Words that look like <u>this</u> can be found in the glossary on page 24.

Ted

Hello! My name's Ellie, and this is my pet dog, Ted. He's six years old. Dogs are my favorite animal because they're great to cuddle, and they always want to play!

Ellie →

4

Whether you're thinking about getting a dog, or you've had one for a little while, Ted and I are going to take you through how to look after a dog!

Lead the way, Ted!

Getting a Dog

Getting a dog and looking after it means you are going to have a lot of **responsibility**. You will need to feed them, and give them a nice home with a comfy bed and lots of toys!

Puppies need a lot of training!

Rescue centers help dogs find new families.

My family got Ted from a rescue center, but you can get dogs from lots of places. You can get a dog from a breeder. This is someone who keeps dogs to **mate** them.

Home

Dogs live in your house with you. They love being around their family and they enjoy exploring, so living alongside you at home is best for them.

At home, dogs need a lot of the same things that you do. They need their own bed, their own place to sit, and lots of toys!

Bed

Don't forget the cuddles, too!

Couch

Toy

Playtime

For dogs, the best part of the day can be going for a walk. They need a place to run, play, and, most importantly, go to the bathroom!

Dogs need lots of exercise!

There are lots of fun games you can play with your dog at the park. Ted's favorite game is fetch. I throw his ball as far as I can, and he brings it back to me.

Dogs love games with balls or sticks.

Food

Dogs, like people, need a **balanced diet**. Dry dog food, called kibble, contains all the things your dog needs to stay healthy.

Dry
Dog Food

Dog treats help dogs to know when they've done something good.

Your dog might also like to eat some meat, fish, vegetables, and rice. Your vet will tell you what to feed your dog.

Bedtime

When it's time to go to sleep, dogs like to have something comfortable and soft to sleep on. You can set up an area for them to sleep, like on the foot of your bed. Or you could buy them a dog bed from the pet store.

Dogs sleep between 12 and 14 hours a day. Puppies and old dogs sleep for even longer. I think Ted gets so tired because of how much fetch we play at the park!

The Vet

Vets are doctors, but for animals instead of humans!

Sometimes dogs can get sick, just like humans. Dogs that are sick can go see the vet. The vet will do everything they can to help your dog get better again!

One day when I came home, Ted was breathing strangely and couldn't stand up very well. I told my parents and we took him to the vet, who made him all better again!

If you think your dog isn't well, make sure you tell someone.

Growing Up

When dogs get old, they get tired more often and want to play less. It's important to be very gentle with them and make sure they are comfortable.

Even though dogs want to play less when they're old, they still want your attention as much as before. Make sure you sit with them and give them lots of cuddles.

Dogs are very loyal to their owners at all ages.

19

Super Dogs

Dogs have some amazing **abilities** that people don't. Did you know that dogs have a sense of smell up to 100,000 times stronger than a human's?

That means you definitely can't hide those treats for very long!

When it gets dark, dogs can see better than people, too. Their eyes let them see up to five times better in the dark than we can.

You definitely won't win a game of hide-and-seek in the dark!

21

You ♥ and Your Pet

Whether you've got a pet dog or you're about to get one, make sure you take care of them just like Ted and I have taught you!

I'm sure you'll make a great pet owner. Try to think of some fun games you can play with your dog, and most of all, have fun with your furry friend!

GLOSSARY

abilities	the power or skills to do something
balanced diet	when an animal or person gets everything they need from their food
loyal	showing constant support for someone
mate	to produce young with an animal of the same species
responsibility	having tasks that you are expected to do

INDEX